The Three Little Pigs

Retold by Annette Smith

Illustrated by Isabel Lowe

Once upon a time
there were three little pigs.

One day their mother said,
"You are big now.
It is time for you to go
and make your own houses."

So off went
the three little pigs.

The first little pig
made his house of straw.

The second little pig
made his house of sticks.

But the third little pig
worked all day
and made **his** house of bricks.

When the sun went down,
the brick house
was ready to live in.

The next day,
a big bad wolf
came out of the forest.

He saw the house
made of straw.
He looked in the window.

"Little pig, little pig,
let me come in," he called.

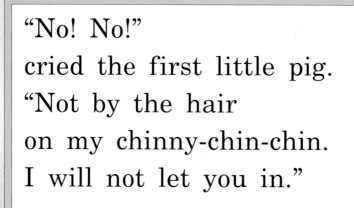

"No! No!"
cried the first little pig.
"Not by the hair
on my chinny-chin-chin.
I will not let you in."

"Then I'll huff, and I'll puff,
and I'll blow your house in,"
said the big bad wolf.

So he huffed, and he puffed, and he **blew** the house in.

The first little pig
ran as fast as he could
to the house made of sticks.

"Help," he cried. "Let me in!
The big bad wolf is coming."

The wolf looked in the window.
"Little pigs, little pigs,
let me come in," he called.

"No! No!"
cried the second little pig.
"Not by the hair
on my chinny-chin-chin.
I will not let you in."

So the wolf huffed,
and he puffed,
and he **blew** the house in.

The two little pigs ran
as fast as they could
to the house made of bricks.

"Help," they cried. "Let us in!
The big bad wolf is coming."
They ran inside,
and the third little pig
locked the door.

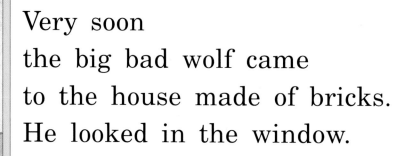

Very soon
the big bad wolf came
to the house made of bricks.
He looked in the window.

"Little pigs, little pigs,
let me come in," he called.

"No! No!"
cried the third little pig.
"Not by the hair
on my chinny-chin-chin.
I will not let you in."

So the wolf huffed,
and he puffed,
and he **huffed**, and he **puffed**,
but he could **not** blow
the house in.

Then the big bad wolf
jumped up onto the roof.
He started to climb
down the chimney!

But the third little pig
was ready for the wolf.
He had a big pot of hot water
on the fire.

He took off the lid,
just in time.
The big bad wolf
fell down the chimney
and into the pot.

And that was the end
of the big bad wolf.

A play
The Three Little Pigs

People in the play

 Narrator

 Mother Pig

 First Little Pig

 Second Little Pig

 Third Little Pig

 Big Bad Wolf

Narrator

Once upon a time,
there were three little pigs.
They lived with their mother,
in a little house.

Mother Pig

You are growing up.
It is time for you to go
and make your own houses.

Third Little Pig *(waving)*

Good-bye!
Good-bye, Mother!

Narrator

So off went the three little pigs.
The first little pig
found some straw.

First Little Pig

This straw will make
a good house.
I will make my house
out of straw.

Second Little Pig (*waving*)

Good-bye, Brother!

Third Little Pig (*waving*)

Let's go on down the road.

Narrator

Soon the second little pig
found some sticks.

Second Little Pig

These sticks will make
a good house.
I'm going to make my house
out of sticks.

Third Little Pig *(waving)*

Good-bye, Brother.
I will go on down the road.

Narrator

The third little pig walked on.
He found some bricks.

Third Little Pig

These bricks will make
a very good house.
I'm going to make my house
out of bricks.

Narrator

The third little pig
worked and worked all day.

Third Little Pig

The sun is going down,
and now my house
is ready to live in.

Narrator

The next day,
a big bad wolf
came out of the forest.
He saw the house
made of straw.
He went up to the window.

Big Bad Wolf

Little pig, little pig,
let me come in.

First Little Pig

No! No!
Not by the hair
on my chinny-chin-chin.
I will not let you in.

Big Bad Wolf

Then, I'll huff, and I'll puff,
and I'll blow your house in.
Huff! Puff!

Narrator

And he huffed, and he puffed,
and he **blew** the house in.

First Little Pig

The big bad wolf will get me.
I will have to run
to my brother's house.

Narrator

The first little pig
got to his brother's house,
just in time.

First Little Pig

Help me! Help me, Brother!
Let me in!
The big bad wolf is coming.

Second Little Pig

Come in! Come in!
The big bad wolf
will not get you in here.

Narrator

The wolf came to the house
made of sticks.
He looked in the window.

Big Bad Wolf

Little pigs, little pigs,
let me come in.

Second Little Pig

No! No!
Not by the hair
on my chinny-chin-chin.
I will not let you in.

Big Bad Wolf

Then I'll huff, and I'll puff,
and I'll **blow** your house in.
Huff! Puff! **Huff! Puff!**

Narrator

And he huffed, and he puffed,
and he **blew** the house in.

First Little Pig

Come on!
The wolf is blowing the house in.
We must run
to our brother's house.

Second Little Pig

Help us! Help us, Brother!
Let us in.
The wolf is coming.

Third Little Pig

Come in! Come in!
I will lock the door!

Big Bad Wolf

Little pigs, little pigs,
let me come in.

Third Little Pig

No! No!
Not by the hair
on my chinny-chin-chin.
I will **not** let you in.

Big Bad Wolf

Then I'll huff, and I'll puff,
and I'll **blow** your house in.
Huff! Puff! **Huff! Puff!**
HUFF! PUFF!

First Little Pig

The big bad wolf
cannot blow **this** house in.

Big Bad Wolf

I will climb down the chimney.

Second Little Pig

Here he comes!
He's coming down the chimney.

Third Little Pig

The water in this pot
is very hot.
I'll take the lid off,
and he will fall into it.

First Little Pig

Look out! Here he comes!

Second Little Pig

He's in the pot!

Third Little Pig

Quick! Put the lid on!

Narrator

And that was the end
of the big bad wolf.